Everything
is
easy-going

(Know Your Response To Every Situation)

BHAVI SHAH

This book is dedicated to YOU.

Yes you, holding this book in your hands. May these pages bring you peace, wonder, gratitude and a place to belong.

Being the only purpose for one and all;

May my words enlightens you with love, prayers and blessings, you are able to give and receive.

CONTENTS

ACKNOWLEDGEMENTS

Writing this book has been an incredible journey, and I am deeply grateful to everyone who has supported me along the way. First and foremost, I want to thank my family for their unwavering love, encouragement, and belief in me, even when I doubted myself. Your patience, understanding, and emotional support have been my anchor throughout this process.

To my friends, thank you for your honesty, laughter, and inspiration. Your words of wisdom and perspective have often been the guiding light; I needed when faced with challenges, and your encouragement to share my insights with others has been invaluable.

I owe a debt of gratitude to the publishing house, my editor and team, whose feedback and expertise transformed this book into what it is today. Your commitment to excellence and your attention to detail have shaped this project in ways I cannot fully express.

I would also like to acknowledge the many teachers, mentors, thought leaders and greatest authors whose work has inspired me.

Super grateful for the words of enlightenment by Gurudev Sri Sri Ravi Shankar, Rhonda Byrne and Joseph Murphy.

Your contributions to personal growth and self-development through your words have made a lasting impact on my own life, and I hope this book can pass some of that wisdom forward.

To the readers: you are the reason this book exists. I hope that the words on these pages resonate with you, help you grow, and provide the insights you need to navigate your own path. Thank you for trusting me with your time and attention—I truly hope this work serves you well.

Finally, I want to express my deep gratitude to everyone who has walked beside me in this journey—whether for a short while or a long stretch. Every conversation, every shared moment, and every piece of advice has contributed to the creation of this book. This is as much your work as it is mine.

With sincere thanks,

ADV. BHAVI SHAH

Gratefully grateful!

A happy mind attracts happiness;
A kind mind attracts kindness;
A positive mind attracts positivity;
A healthy mind attracts healthy energy;
A brave mind attracts bravery,
but;
A grateful mind attracts abundance in every field of life.

– Bhav9_thefeels

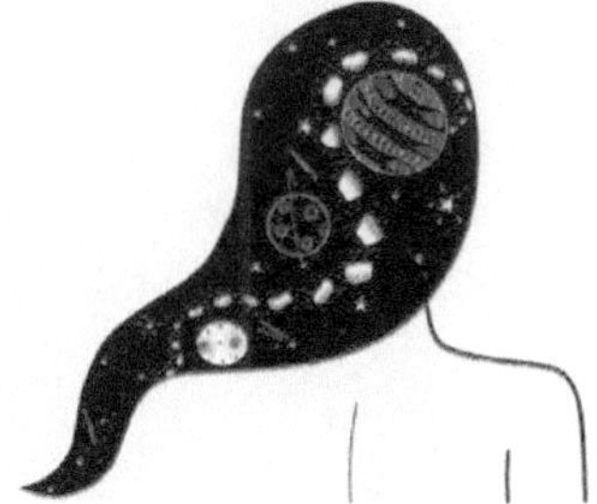

INTRODUCTION

Welcome to Everything is easy-going: A journey of self-care. I am thrilled to embark on this journey with you as we explore the pathways to growth, self-love and fulfilment together.

In our fast paced and ever changing world, it's easy to feel overwhelmed, lost, or stuck in the same old patterns. We all face challenges, setbacks, and moments of doubt along the way. But within each of us lies the power to rise above adversity, embrace change, and create a life that reflects our deepest desires and aspirations.

This book is a set of experiences and a road map for unlocking your full potential and living a life of purpose, passion and joy. Drawing from my own experiences, insights, and years of study in personal development, psychology, and spirituality, I have crafted a comprehensive guide to help you navigate life's challenges with resilience, courage and grace.

Throughout these pages, you'll discover practical strategies, transformative exercises and empowering principles to help you:

1.   Cultivate self-awareness and mindfulness to enhance your emotional well-being.

2.   Overcome limiting beliefs, fears and self-doubt that holds you back from achieving your goals.

3.   Harness the power of intention, visualization and goal setting to manifest your dreams into reality.

4.   Cultivate healthy habits, routines and gratitude rituals that support your physical, mental and spiritual well-being.

5.   Foster meaningful connections and nourishing relationships that enrich your life and bring you joy.

6.   Embrace change, uncertainty and adversity as opportunities for growth, learning and self-discovery.

Each chapter of this book is designed to guide you on a self-care journey with love, prayers and high hopes turning into blessings. Through introspection, reflection and actions, you will uncover your unique strengths, passions and purpose, and step into the fullest expression of who you are meant to be.

This is a simple book with simpler words and simple life experiences helping to get much simple ways of understanding of how to turn your life as simple as it can be.

I invite you to approach this book with an open mind and a willingness to explore new possibilities, Whether you are seeking clarity, inspiration, or practical guidance, I hope that EVERYTHING IS EASY-GOING serves as a trusted companion on your path of understanding self-care.

Together let's embark upon this journey of self-care, love, compassion and growth. Your adventure begins now.

With gratitude and excitement,

Adv. Bhavi Shah

The universe talks about
the magic and the power it holds,
that can really mould your life
according to what you pray and urge for.

— Bhav9_thefeels

UNFOLDING MAGIC

In a world that often feels clouded by uncertainty, there is a power in words—an undeniable magic that can heal, uplift, and transform. Words, when spoken with love and intention, can invoke blessings and miracles, weaving a tapestry of light and hope into the lives of those who believe.

There is one friend of mine, who found herself lost in a maze of sorrow. She had tried everything to heal her broken heart and restore her peace, but the weight of grief seemed unbearable. One day, while seeking comfort, she came to me for venting out and feel better. I just heard her patiently and then spoke of trust, of miracles, and the power of prayer which you will get to know later in this book. Without fully understanding how, she felt the stirring of something deep within her—something that whispered, "Trust."

With nothing left to lose, she repeated the words of that prayer I taught her, over and over: "I trust in the love of the universe, and I trust that blessings are already on their way to me. Miracles unfold at the perfect moment, and I am open to receiving them. I am worthy of love, of peace, and of all the beautiful things life has to offer." And as she spoke those words aloud, she felt an overwhelming sense of warmth and light surrounding her.

Days passed, and slowly, the heaviness that had once consumed her began to lift. Her heart, once shattered, started to heal. The universe, responding to her faith and trust, began to bring unexpected blessings—her other friends reaching out, opportunities knocking, and a deep, unwavering sense of peace settling within her.

Never say no to any opportunity even if it feels impossible to attain. Make room in your heart for the same. The universe will unfold the best possible way to get you through it with the least resistance. I have been regularly using this method and getting the results effortlessly. Let me tell you how this happens through a very simple story of mine. Once, I was so occupied in my studies and I wanted one of the book lying on my desk from the other room. I just planted the desire in my heart for having that book without getting up as it would break my concentration. It naturally happened within 10 minutes of believing that I'll have that; by my mother who just handed it to me even without asking as she was passing by the room. I have been blessed in all aspects of my life but I started feeling more blessed when I understood the real meaning of being grateful and believing that nature is always working in my favour without even asking. Unfolding miracles is simply trusting that everything will be done for you with complete ease. All the luxuries whether materialistic or non-materialistic, I attain in my life is simply by unfolding the magic with gratitude, prayers, love and trust altogether.

So, try to be like us who dared to trust in the power of words, experienced the magic that unfolds when love, faith, and intention are united. Miracles don't always come in grand gestures, but in quiet moments of surrender and trust. It is in the simple act of speaking words with faith that blessings take root and miracles bloom.

As you read this, know that the same power lies within you. Trust in the words that carry love, faith, and hope. Say them with your whole heart, and allow the universe to guide you toward the miracles you seek. Hence, when you trust in the magic of words, blessings follow, and miracles manifest in ways you could never imagine.

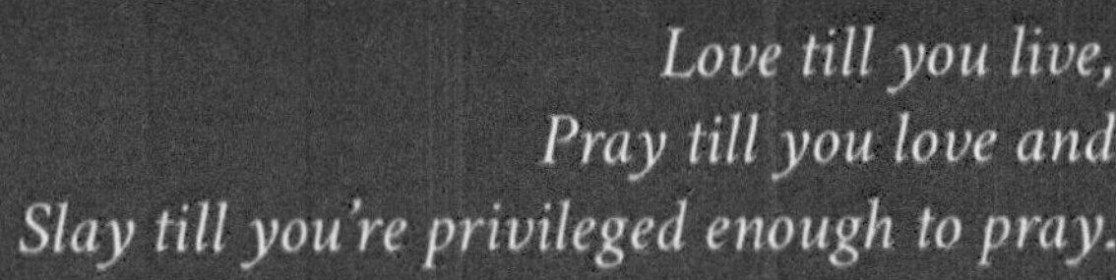

Love till you live,
Pray till you love and
Slay till you're privileged enough to pray.

— Bhav9_thefeels

LOVE, PRAY AND SLAY

TURNAROUND TO GRATITUDE OR TURNAROUND TO UNIVERSE.

– IT HEALS!

Think of the possibilities, go around and try to understand the directions given by the universe to turn your dreams into reality.

Accept the facts and acknowledge your fulfilled desires to feel the immense joy of satisfaction.

I once had a big unwanted fight with one of my loved one. And that led me to a traumatized situation which seem to be unhealed and impossible to sort. I can say I was at my lowest as little things matters the most to me and I believe this to be an issue with many people. I tried out number of things to get the negativity out of my mind but the most important of all was reading books that can help to get my mind stronger and develop positive feelings which were totally out of my mind. Certainly, it helped; it worked. I chose to read mainly 3 things: THE POWER OF SUBCONSIOUS MIND BY JOSEPH MURPHY, THE MAGIC BY RHONDA BYRNE AND SRI SRI RAVI SHANKAR'S TEACHINGS. And the most crazy and amazing part is the fight resolved by my 2-way efforts i.e. continuous rotation of my desire to get my fight sorted in my subconscious mind and also working on communicating with the other to resolve the misunderstandings that led to this fight. And one of the most important thing to be mentioned here in relevance to this excerpt of my life story is **TO PRAY.**

TO PRAY FOR WHAT YOU WANT, PRAY HARDER. You are going to get it for sure, if you deserve that.

A PRAYER IS A KIND OF EXPRESSION OF YOUR DESIRES WHICH COULD DIRECTLY OR INDIRECTLY WORK FOR GOOD PURPOSE IN THIS WORLD.

PRAY DAILY BUT OFTENLY FOR WHAT YOU NEED.

LET YOUR PRAYERS BE KIND.

LET YOUR PRAYERS BE GENUINE.

LET YOUR PRAYERS BE EFFORTLESS.

LET YOUR PRAYERS BE TRUE.

LET YOUR PRAYERS BE SELFLESS.

Just let god to handle your situations when you just cannot think of any solution to get out of it. It is crazy how the presence of God can completely change your mood and attitude in an instance. One worship song, one whispered prayer, one scripture verse can take you from the absolute worst mind-set to a place of such peace and joy. There is nothing like the presence of God, Because if he made you to face that situation then he must be having the absolute plan to make you wiser, increase your resistance and to build you up to make the correct choices.

Crying your heart out in front of your friends who could just hear and understand the exact suffering you are going through is one of the best way to release and get free. So, you get to think wisely and pray sincerely. Even the prayers of your friends and well-wishers work for you all the time which you are completely unaware about and that's the beauty of prayers or wishes which make smooth working of your life in the world full of selfish people. Also, crying does not make you weak, it shows that you're raw and pure, inside out. Do not take crying as a sign of weakness ever. Because after crying, you develop a higher sense of realisation to get out from any situation that disturbed you or ruined your peace. And take a note, once you're done crying for any reason, do not cry for the same again. In order to protect your peace and intellect, you should get over any particular matter over a reasonable time.

The understanding is simple – YOU CRY BECAUSE YOU LOVE, YOU PRAY BECAUSE YOU LOVE, AND YOU SLAY BECAUSE YOU LOVE, MY LOVE.

Believe in
the working of nature,
the process,
the outcome,
the desire,
the reality,
the dreams and
their fulfilment.
Literally everything.
And most importantly, believe in yourself.

—Bhav9_thefeels

BELIEVE TILL YOU RECEIVE

LIFE IS UNPREDICTABLE, BUT YOUR BELIEF ON TOMMOROW KEEPS YOU MOVING.

An immense and absolute peace of mind is an achievement these days where people are confused and demotivated all the time. People search for motivation and peace these days via videos, clips, thoughts over internet but the real motivation lies within you. It is not just a matter of saying but feeling and experiencing it by your own. And you'll get amazing outputs from your own self attaining and realising the value of contentment.

PRAYERS WORK FOR YOU WHEN YOU'RE CONTENTED. PRAYERS WORK FOR YOU WHEN YOU FEEL BLESSED. PRAYERS WORK FOR YOU WHEN YOU FEEL GRATEFUL.

DO ALL THE GOOD YOU CAN,

BY ALL THE MEANS YOU CAN,

IN ALL THE WAYS YOU CAN,

IN ALL THE PLACES YOU CAN,

AT ALL THE TIMES YOU CAN,

TO ALL THE PEOPLE YOU CAN,

AS LONG AS EVER YOU CAN.

– JOHN WESLEY

Life doesn't goes as per our strategies but as per god's plan.

Uncertainties do hit one and all but our reaction to those is what matters. I heard somewhere that during the hard times try to recall and remember the best of the memories life has given you, it helps to ease the pain right at the moment. Now, let me make you understand how our positive approach to a negative situation can make the situation balanced and convenient. During the times of covid-19 pandemic, economies got hit harder than anyone could ever have thought. People were suffering from pressure and scarcity of jobs and resources to earn a living. Quite the same situation arose in the life of one of our closed ones too. And not because they had not had enough but a negative approach of one of their family members towards the situation made it tough. I have learned that you could only try to modify thought process of anyone for few moments but you just could not change it completely. So, instead try out to rectify that situation at your personal level. I believed and suggested the same. I made sure that I am enough grateful for everything on behalf of that person and did that practice every day. Within a few days a payment was received to them and situation got normal technically and automatically. Make sure that you are genuinely grateful for everything you own or ought to receive in future. This could be life-changing to all those who try out this not only for self but for others too.

Better to get moving on with the trust in the universe, then holding on to what's beyond our control.

BE THE ONE ON WHOM PEOPLE COULD RELY.

Since the school time, I loved to write a lot. But I wasn't aware of my passion towards writing. Life just threw an opportunity to me to understand and work for it. I grabbed it at the right moment and here I am. When I started writing I had no idea of apt. writing forms, structures or anything. I just wrote what I felt. But as it grows, it gives me immense pleasure to pour my heart out, sharing my experiences that could help in bettering the lives and minds of the people who gets to read the same.

Trust the universe with;
Thankfulness for everything,
apology for the missteps,
inspirations from the life experiences and
aspirations for a better future.

— Bhav9_thefeels

INSPIRATION AND ASPIRATION GOES HAND IN HAND

When you inspire someone, you expect them to get aspired to do the rightful. My mother is my inspiration of all the times and I guess most of us would be having the same. From protecting us from a mean world to standing out as a warrior in the same; She made us strong and fearless. She taught us good or I can say the best things to get a structured and peaceful life. And most importantly doing good and praying for the well-being of each and every one out there. Since childhood I saw her doing unconditional help and prayers for all. And this is one of the best personality trait one could adopt for a satisfied living. As now, she is getting older with the passing days; sometimes she gets disturbed too where she cannot hold on her anger but her teachings itself helps to set the situation right. I try to make her remember her own beautiful thoughts to get her back on track calmly and easily.

Since, I aspire to be like my mom but I am inspired to be a better version.

And my version goes like –

"Getting so inspired with being thankful that I never get a chance to be sorry is what I aspire."

But can't deny that life has many ways of overwhelming us where we can lose our true senses. And for that, you need to acquire this as well.

Inspiration and **aspiration** can be rooted with the simple yet powerful words: *"Thank You"* and *"Sorry."*

These words shape our growth, relationships, and the ways we navigate life.

Inspiration through Gratitude ("Thank You")

When we express gratitude, we acknowledge the good in our lives.

Saying *"Thank You"* inspires us to appreciate what we have, motivating us to give back, work harder, and spread kindness.

Gratitude fuels positive energy, attracting more reasons to be thankful. It inspires others, as appreciation creates a ripple effect—when we acknowledge someone's efforts, they feel valued and encouraged.

Aspiration through Apology ("Sorry")

Apologizing is not just about accepting or admitting a mistake; it's about self-awareness and the desire to improve.

Saying *"Sorry"* shows humility, helping us learn from our actions and aspire to be better.

It strengthens relationships, as true aspirations come from meaningful connections.

Recognizing our shortcomings pushes us toward self-growth and a higher version of ourselves.

Balancing the Two

When we live with gratitude (*Thank You*), we stay inspired. When we take responsibility (*Sorry*), we keep aspiring. Together, they shape a life of growth, wisdom, and fulfilment.

SAYING SORRY IS GOOD BUT SAYING THANKYOU IS THE BEST.

You would never get a chance to be sorry if you're always thankful. It's quite tough to be in the practice of being thankful all the time but it's not impossible. You need to cultivate the habit with each passing day, adding it to your routine, till you find yourself amazed by the number of times you feel grateful or being grateful in complete 24 hours.

YOUR MIND IS YOUR LEADER, INJECT IT WITH POSITIVITY. YOUR FEET ARE YOUR FOUNDATION, WALK WITH PURPOSE. AND YOUR HEART IS YOUR STAMP, MAKE IT BEAUTIFUL.

– TENE EDWARDS, WALK WITH WINGS.

As you train your mind to be in constant awareness of being grateful. It will never lead you down.

What matters the most
is how pure your heart is.

— Bhav9_thefeels

DO NOT WAIT FOR SOMEONE TO BE KIND, BE KIND

There are many instances where you expect someone to be kind or good to you or others. But not everyone has a heart like you neither you can amend it in the way you want. KINDNESS IS THE BIGGEST VIRTUE OF ALL. Try to think and wish good for the people nearby or far away from you. Trust me the power of wishing good for others would be one of the most satisfying things on the earth. People are so indulged in their own chores that they often forget to pray even for their own self. And praying for others simply would help those in need. When you pray for others, you get the instant access in developing the good thoughts by your own in any situation. I would prescribe it to practice this on daily basis at any of the events where you feel genuine need to pray for someone. Like, you could pray for someone begging out there, for any accident victims, for any ambulance passing by, for the animals around you and as such. Just do it with all your heart and get your good karma score at a higher level instantly. Do not wait for any opportunity to pray. Do it. Do it deeply.

I READ SOMEWHERE THAT –

"GENEROUS PEOPLE ARE GENEROUS WITH EVERYTHING, INCLUDING THEIR EMOTIONS."

And this is for all those who could use their generosity for anything to heal any kind of situation.

Sometimes miracles are just good people with kind heart.

It's amazing what you can get done if you quietly, clearly and authoritatively demand it.

– Meryl Streep

Demanding doesn't depend on the basis of needs and wants; it's the imbalance of mind and heart that arises any demand in particular. Fulfilled demands particularly of the materialistic things are obviously satisfactory but just for few moments or few days or may be few years but not more than that. But in case of those non materialistic, precious things like demanding luck, good wishes and happiness from the universe for one and all would bring you the utmost joy that could be kept forever. Even after a long period of time, you would be sitting idle, relaxing and if you would be thinking about all the prayers you made for others will bring you peace. You will realise about the gift of giving in true sense then. You will feel proud. You will feel complete. I wish that may you all do practice the prayers and feel the sincere joy.

If god closes all the doors in your life. It's certainly a redirection. He sees the potential in you to be the warrior all by your own. You are capable of surviving without everything and everyone. As you try to live all by your own, you will find out the ways to fit in your own space without any acknowledgement. As we all know the famous saying – if god closes one door, he opens another. And even if he does not, he makes sure that he has the right choice and direction for you at that point of time. When you cannot find any solution or anything for the uncertain event occurring in your life; just bless the situation. Bless the person or persons nearby you who made you stand at that point. Bless the circumstances that led you to witness that situation and bless those who are standing beside you for more or little of help. You can easily cope up with the hardest of situations by doing this. I can assure you this by my own experience of letting go of the tough situation just by blessing it. When you sincerely practice this, you will get an instant smile on your face. It is the sign of practicing the genuine blessing and healing. And that's where you have chosen you over everyone and everything that is passing by you. You are in complete stage of awareness regarding your power of healing and sustainability.

It's not important to be right. It's important to be true.

INSTEAD OF TRYING TO FIT IN, LIVE THE
LIFE THAT FITS YOU.

— J.IRONWOOD

WE ARE AN AMALGM OF THOUGHTS ATTACHED TO EMOTIONS THAT SET UNCONSCIOUS INTENTIONS BEHIND EVERYTHING WE DO.

When you are true to your own-self, you are in power to think and do the rightful for everyone around you. There comes the time where you are not up to the mark or up to where you want to be but that is not the final stage. Life throws innumerable challenges at you just to make you stronger, bolder and harder. You are capable of overcoming and over powering the situation or any circumstance by having a clear vision about your own self. Reaching out to the correct options or the solutions is done with a mere thought process where things get unfold for your betterment. You become your saviour with just a thought of being or reaching a healthier state of mind, of body, of heart and of all the emotions as well.

Every time you speak kindly to yourself, your mind learns to trust you. Keep going. As kindness starts from self and leads to more of the same for the world.

Give yourself time to
understand, heal and grow.
Let yourself slow down
and
get the right idea of
what really matters.

— Bhav9_thefeels

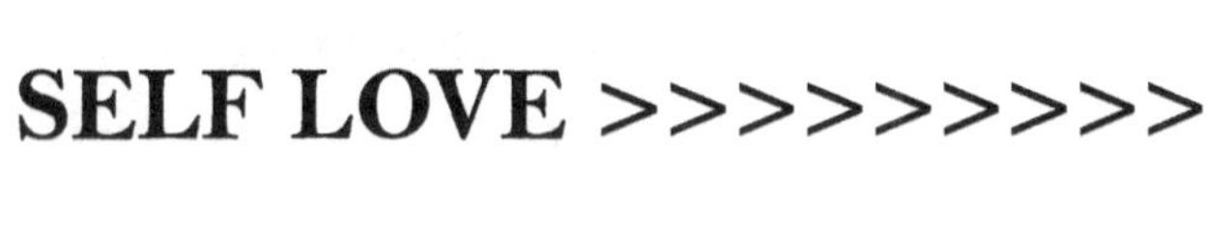

SELF LOVE >>>>>>>>>>

JUST AS A CAR REQUIRES SERVICING OR MAINTENANCE AFTER A CERTAIN PERIOD OF TIME, SIMILARLY OUR BODY AND MIND REQUIRES MAINTENANCE TOO.

This perception is the first stage of self-love which is majorly required by everyone.

People undergo situations like cheating, misunderstanding, jealousy, fraud etc. which brings miseries and sorrows in many lives altogether and thus, they need to cut these negative elements for thyself. In order to relinquish these feelings, one must cultivate the habit of self-love.

MORE THE SELF LOVE, MORE THE LOVE FOR OTHERS. MORE THE GOOD THOUGHTS FOR OWNSELF, MORE THE GOOD THOUGHTS FOR OTHERS.

Therefore, when you starts developing positivity for yourself, you will be more positive for others and for the situations that tests our power to stay positive and calm. Invest in yourself. And with this phrase, I mean and suggest doing the inner work. That is choosing the things which literally makes you happy and brings you at peace.

Ok, let me tell you about the practices that helps me to stay at peace.

1. Dancing on my favourite songs.

2. Listening music. (Whatever it feels like at that moment)

3. Creating art. (Sketching, drawing and writing)

4. Reading.

5. But not at all scrolling the reels.

You can choose and make your own list. BUT MAKE SURE YOU DO. Because in this much happening world, constantly evolving and changing. You are going to need some things to escape from the outer source to be at peace and to make yourself happy which is directly related to the aura you carry. And of course, everyone wants their aura clear, calm and strong.

Here are some suggestions for you to practice that could bring you to peace.

1. Stay in the nature

2. If you want, click pictures of anything you love around you.

3. Hug people with whom you are comfortable.

4. Lie down and think of all the happy moments. (Ignore the past, present or future)

You could add anything which suits you better but make sure your thoughts are calm and clear in any practice you do.

Trust me these are definitely going to help you.

Wishing you a happy self-love practice!

Cherish the moments before
it turns out to be memories.

— Bhav9_thefeels

FORGIVE, FORGET AND HEAL

Hold on to nothing, to survive everything, easily.
WHY DO PEOPLE SAY FORGIVE AND FORGET?

Our lives being super busy and happening where we don't actually get time to hold on to something whether it is good or bad. According to human nature, people celebrate happiness for a few days but mourns at any loss for longer period of time. It shows that the ultimate need of human psychology is to understand the concept of letting go much deeply and also practicing it efficiently. Forgiving and forgetting seems an easy task but it's harder than one could think of. As it is said – "You keep forgiving someone until you un-love them." But the part which needs to be understood the most is one must forgive and forget for their own benefit. It takes a lot of strength for letting things go. But this will make you powerful and help you conquer your mind with what is the best for you.

As soon as we shift our response to any situation in a positive way, we tend to switch it to good memory securing it from turning into a bad experience.

Try to find out the good in the misery. Feel grateful for the happening of that particular event which lead to the misery. Look at it as the opportunity to get wiser. Be thankful for each lessons you got. And there is your win waiting for you to understand and accept the god's plan.

EGO SAYS,

"Once everything falls into place, I'll feel peace."

SPIRIT SAYS,

"Find your peace, and then everything will fall into the place."

– MARIANNE WILLIAMSON

WALK WITH GRACE

It requires a deep sense of acceptance when you understand, you are more than enough, not just for your own self but for all the people around you.

If you are unable to find the blessings on the step that you are currently stuck on, be prepared to live a life of misery.

The thing is our minds are so used to get stuck over a particular matter or situation that we are unable to move on easily. We need all the answers to our why, when, how so much that we often tend to forget that we have got a life ahead of the same. Technically, if you love yourself enough, letting go is quite easy. And by letting go here means to get over the negative remark of any situation you're facing instead try to have a positive outlook since you need this to take your life in the right direction.

You are capable of forgiving and forgetting only if you have accepted the situation with complete grace and made peace with it. In this way you heal, and with healing, you bring the blessing for yourself. And with the blessing comes the power to get through anything with complete forgiveness and letting go.

HEALING REQUIRES IT ALL.

HEALING REQUIRES FORGIVENESS.

HEALING REQUIRES LETTING GO.

HEALING REQUIRES WISDOM.

HEALING REQUIRES LOVE.

HEALING REQUIRES KINDNESS.

AND WITH ALL THESE; HEALING BRINGS PEACE.

In such manner, you would not only heal yourself but the world too. And as we already know, this world needs more of it.

Happiness lies in giving.
Clearly and evidently.

— Bhav9_thefeels

HAPPINESS COMES TO THOSE WHO DESIRES FOR OTHERS HAPPINESS

Only when you walk with grace will you taste the sweetness of happiness.

– TENE EDWARDS, WALK WITH WINGS.

This is one of my life rules(can be called as lifesaving rule) where each and every time I think of happiness for others, blessings for others, being grateful for fulfilment of other's desires and as such. This truly makes me happy from within and brings an instant smile on my face. I practice this almost daily and at every such moment when I am free or at peace. Trust me, you will feel the genuine happiness just by praying and praising any-body, any-where, anytime. Make it a habit and you're not going to regret this ever. Start practicing it by praying for your parents (I know everybody does this already but not on a regular basis) or your closed one who are in need. The outcome of this beautiful habit will bring you wonders. As said – "A good heart can bring things into your life that all the money in the world couldn't obtain." So, have faith and keep praying.

There are literally many of my life experiences where I felt that the power of manifesting or you can say praying for others turned out to be so magical.

It's not like others getting the desired results because I prayed for them but it's more like their hard work + their trust in my prayers or the effortless manifestations I do. And this is all possible because of the genuine, sincere intention and all the love and gratitude practice and moreover trusting the process, that helps me to avail the desired results to them or I can say to make them happy with what they want to achieve.

PRACTICING GENEROSITY IS SIMPLE. JUST MAKE IT A MOTTO IN YOUR LIFE.

And trust me this experience is so satisfying and peaceful that you would not want to miss out on this.

So, this turn out to be the understanding for – HAPPINESS COMES TO THOSE WHO DESIRES FOR OTHERS HAPPINESS.

LIVING UPTO OUR IDEAL SELF GIVES SATISFACTION. LETTING GO OF OUR IDEAL SELF GIVES LIBERATION.

– ALEXANDER DEN HEIJER

The day to day life chores keeps you busy and helps you in avoiding the odds but you cannot neglect them completely.

BEING BUSY IS NOT THE SOLUTION TO ALL OF YOUR PROBLEMS BUT CHOOSING THE RIGHT TIME AND THE METHOD TO COPE UP IS - Stop wondering over it frequently and rather give it some time when you are at peace and able to understand what needs to be done.

I have read this beautiful piece somewhere –

'Maybe happiness is not about us, as individuals.

Maybe it is not something that arrives into us.

Maybe happiness is felt heading out, not in.

Maybe happiness is not about what we deserve because we're worth it.

Maybe happiness is not about what we can get.

Maybe happiness is about what we already have.

Maybe happiness is about what we can give.

Maybe happiness is not a butterfly we can catch with a net.

Maybe there is no certain way to be happy.

Maybe there are only maybes.'

If (as EMILY DICKINSON said) 'forever – is composed of Nows– maybe, the nows are made of maybes.' Maybe the point of life is to give up certainty and to embrace life's beautiful uncertainty.

Soulful connections are rare but are there;
If you find one, keep and preserve.
Life gives second chances but not every time.

— Bhav9_thefeels

VALUE YOUR LOVED
ONES UNTIL THEY
ARE WITH YOU.
EXPEREINCING LOSS FOR
UNDERSTANDING THEIR
VALUE IS ANOTHER
LEVEL OF STUPIDITY

Every time it is not necessary to show your anger, pain or any kind of sorrow with the silence or ignorance. It requires communication and understanding to sort and heal. With the experiences of loss of lives of closed ones or the silent treatment with anyone who used to be quite an important part of my life, I got to know that your love is the only thing that stays with you, nothing else matters, nothing.

THERE IS NOTHING WITHOUT COMMUNICATION. SO, HOW DO YOU THINK WILL THE LOVE SURVIVE WITHOUT THE GENUINE WORDLY EXPRESSION?

In any of your relationships whether it is with your mother, father, sibling, friends, lovers, relatives, cousins, and spouse or in laws; the first and the foremost factor that is present is love.

When you feel love, you realise its type – authentic or not. But sometimes actions could be fake in order to fulfil the responsibility or to come up with the expectations, one keeps doing everything that is required for any relation. But the words that comes out of love is easily identifiable and experienced. You can feel the most calming and peaceful vibes when you get to hear those from a loved one or from any one you expect.

And as long as we are here on this planet; I believe and would suggest you to offer love, compassion and support to your loved ones and everyone else around you in need by any means. Because world truly needs more of that.

Also, extend deepest gratitude for being around your loved ones for any amount of time or some quality time nature has provided you. Being living in the borrowed time, valuing the presence of anyone who loves you unconditionally is one of the biggest understanding, one needs. As, not everyone gets to be around their loved ones they wish for.

"I pray no one gets to get through the feeling of getting away from their loved ones."

Prayer is not

something you do to wish for anything or when
thanking for granted wishes;

But

Prayer is

something we can offer to have gratitude for everything
that has already been rendered to us without even
asking.

— Bhav9_thefeels

PRAYERS ARE THE
SYNONYMS OF THE
MIRACLES

Prayers! Prayers! Prayers!

Anxiety is preventive. JUST HELP YOURSELF OR OTHERS WHO ARE IN NEED, WITH PRAYERS.

Blocking the negative energies to surround anyone who suffers any of anxiety or depression. Clearing the energies to heal the sufferers is the kindness or help anybody can offer to anyone who is suffering from the same. They won't seek you for help but you have to analyse and support them without letting them know. Since, everyone has got energies and vibrations, one can use the same for the good cause, if he or she can. Because universe has set a particular goal for everyone on the planet. You just need to find yours and work for it, may be it could help someone in need. May be you could prove to be a blessing for someone who was not even expecting anything. May be you could save a heart which is completely broken. There are many more such may be's. If you are able to read this, you are one of the maybes who is here to offer kindness and prayers for everyone in need. And even you got a hint about the goal, god has set for you. So, get started with the theories of love, gratitude, kindness and prayers. YOU are a saviour, YOU are a blessing. The world needs you. Your realisation of the same could bring the change. You can bring revolutionary changes just with your thoughts. And by now you may have already witnessed the same. Keep spending and collecting love, smiles and thankyous'.

AS KINDNESS IS A FORM OF PRAYER TOO.

People usually ask me, what is the perfect love language?

And according to me or what I do is –

"PRAYERS"

"PRAYERS"

"Yes, I pray for the ones I love. Their name comes into my prayers automatically. I pray for their health, wealth, well-being and happiness. I pray for their families' health, wealth and happiness. I always do, unconditionally and selflessly."

And those who are close to me or know me well can relate and may be smiling right now while reading this. ☺

We need to be
so in love with everything
around us that
it gets easier to understand
that we have been provided
a lot more than we deserve from
the nature.

— *Bhav9_thefeels*

YOUR WISH, MY COMMAND – SAYS THE UNIVERSE (NO MATTER THE KIND OF WISH, GOOD OR BAD; WISH WISELY)

You just need to have sheer confidence on the process of achieving all your wishes. As it is said – "the universe always falls in love with the stubborn heart". I have been through much of the rough times smoothly because I trusted in the process of universe and it's nature of giving. But make sure your wishes much be of such kind that could hold much of the good value to you and even to others. It that should not bring any trouble for others. As kind hearts are loved by the god and the nature too and vice-versa/or the other way round.

"Take control or charge of your mind and heart." – An easy proverb been used to guide someone but no one explains or demonstrates that how to achieve the same.

Since, I have been through the same confusion, I could help you with what helped me to strive this control. It is actually not as easy as it states in the statement. You need to acquire the sincerity in everything you will be doing for yourself. You have to relate, what you want with what you'll be getting. You need to discuss the same with your parents, siblings or friends. You need to make sure that no matter what you're trusting in the timing and process of the universe. You need to back it up with positive intention and genuine prayers.

But I ensure you, the outcome will definitely be as desired or may be more than you've hoped.

You ever stopped and thought – "Wow! I prayed for this. It's here. It's happening." That is the very moment of the realisation of extreme gratification. It doesn't happens all of a sudden but with consistent prayers and efforts simultaneously. As universe loves to provide, always.

Be insanely protective
about yourself,
your emotions,
your mental and physical health,
your aura and like for
everything that includes
or involves you.

— Bhav9_thefeels

YOU ARE YOUR OWN SAVIOUR

It is a series of tough decisions.

Decision to be more disciplined, to address your recurring toxic thoughts, to prioritise your mental health and to put your happiness over your history.

To get started with something:

1. It may be a guided meditation.

2. Listening peaceful or spiritual music

3. Healing by being in the nature. (Surrounded by nature and have a good communication with moon, plants, birds or whosoever you wish to.)

4. Sending love through vibes, thoughts or may be over texts or calls.

5. Forgiving everyone. (With all your heart)

6. Apologising to everyone. (If you cannot apologise them directly, do it in your heart with full emotions and love.)

Nothing but all the love.

People keep saying – "Actions speaks louder than words." But if we analyse, people are thirsty of hearing loving, kind and caring words for securing mental satisfaction that merely loving gestures cannot do.

Loving is easy, proving is tough.

And those who are in literal need of love won't understand the gestures merely because reassurances are the words, those kind words someone needs to hear or to read or in any other form that could satisfy their hearts.

We totally rely on people to make us feel loved. And if we don't get enough of the same, we feel the lack, we feel abandonment. In order to keep our hearts safe, we really need to be our own saviour.

So, all in all what you expect to get from others in form of love is all you need to give to yourself.

YOU are above all and everyone in your life. Understand your needs carefully. Love yourself. Tell all the words of love, affection and kindness to yourself. Practice it daily. Write in and keep it around you, so you can read it regularly. I am sharing here the affirmations I have hanged around me:

I AM BLESSED

I AM WORTHY

I AM LOVED

I AM STRONG

I AM LOVING

I AM VALUED

I AM MAGIC

I AM FAVOURED

I AM KIND

I AM GUIDED

I AM PROTECTED

I AM GRATEFUL

And do not just read these, but feel and understand that you already are. Because at the end you're your only saviour.

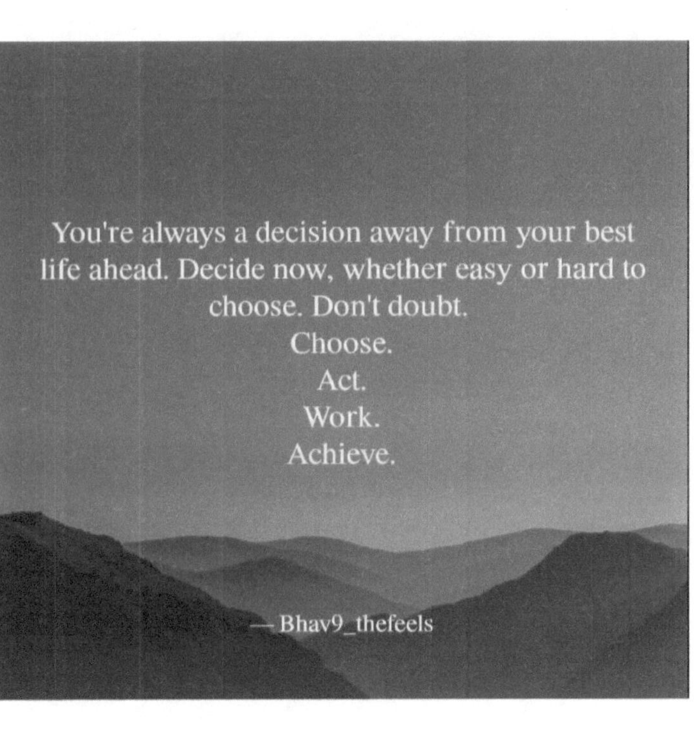

You're always a decision away from your best life ahead. Decide now, whether easy or hard to choose. Don't doubt.
Choose.
Act.
Work.
Achieve.

— Bhav9_thefeels

MINDFUL WITHOUT BEING OUT OF MIND

Let's talk about the day to day life.

Your parents, your spouse, your kids, your complete family, your friends, the people you meet, the people who work for you, the people who teaches you, the people you follow, the people who follows you, the neighbours, the strangers, the people with whom you had an eye contact, the people you think of and the people who think of you. Each and every one of them is related to you with some or the other reason which you may or may not be knowing.

But what you need to do is to have peace with every one of them in your head and eventually you will witness the same around you without doing anything. Just bless them in whichever way, they need or you want but do it.

You will be rewarded with what you have never even imagined.

I will tell you one of my ways to give you an idea of how you could practice to bless every-one in your day to day life.

So, what I do is –

Wishing in the heart for the good health, wealth and peace for any number of people at a particular point of time. (But try to be particular with limited no. of persons up to 4 at a particular point of time.) And as I move out of the house and see different types of people, I pray for their happiness as well inside my heart even if I know them or not.

It's my instinct that has been so deeply involved in practicing gratitude and praying, that I have developed this habit. And thus it happens naturally that I do such practices effortlessly.

So, just try to be natural with your thoughts and be in peace. You will eventually develop this habit as well.

I have got to realise much about working of minds and instincts. To let your mind work according to you or to let yourself work according to your mind is all up to you and your way of living. If you want your mind to work according to you, you simply need a pause, a hold, a moment of calmness to let it function in the way which is beneficial for you.

As Darius Foroux said in one of his books – COMMIT TO STOP THINKING USELESS THINGS AND START TAKING CONTROL OF YOUR MIND.

Life excerpts or experiences are the best way to explain anything to anyone. Because your mind works and reacts to any situation according to the choices previously taken or chosen and with the end results of the same. For example, you learn from the mistakes of your own or may be of your friends or your peers or your colleagues or by hearing experiences of any one, you're mostly surrounded with. And with those learnings your mind reacts to any situation that comes up to you. Since, experience makes one wiser but only if one is willing to learn from it. Making the best choice is generally the job of our mind but what you want out of any situation usually relies on your instincts or your gut feeling.

It is generally the divine or the signs of universe that shows you the right way or the right option for you. All you need is to be patient with any situation and to understand the same, it is quite tough to be patient at the time of adversities but the process of nature always works on your favour. It's just that some realises it sooner and some later.

Relax! LET GO ALL OF YOUR THOUGHTS!

Make sure your brain is in your control and make an imagination of what you want to receive or have. I assure you, the world will be in your hands if you follow and practice.

PRACTICE KINDNESS.

PRACTICE SUPPORTING.

PRACTICE CONTROLLING.

PRACTICE POSITIVITY.

These practices are not something to be learnt, these are something to be developed. You have got these, you just need to channelize and use it in your daily routine.

YOU WILL BE AMAZED WITH THE RESULTS. (SO AM I, EVERYTIME WHEN I PRACTICE THESE).

Realm of gratitude and connection with the brain, needs to be found out to get the reality check of life and the working of the universe around us.

Protecting your mind from the evil or negative thoughts is the foremost practice you need to develop to pursue the life you desire. Thinking practically, being in this world, without any uncertainty or tough situation is quite impossible but the situation you face in a particular (unpleasant) kind can surely be changed by changing responses through your thought process.

FUNCTIONING YOUR BRAIN TO PROCESS ONLY GOOD THOUGHTS IS THE BEST SOLUTION. (not-so-easy) But yes it is possible if you try and make it a habit in your day to day life. Preserve your thoughts, because it will directly preserve your mind, health, body, money and your whole lifestyle.

Real endeavour lies in maintaining an
innocent and pure heart in this selfish world.

— Bhav9_thefeels

ALL IT NEEDS IS A PURE HEART WITH GENUINE INTENTIONS

It is said – "There is always 2 sides of a coin."

But do know that there is merely a COIN.

The point is of the perception.

It is all about the right and wrong.

It is not always about the differences in thoughts of 2 individuals but sometimes it's about the juggle between the mind and the heart.

There is always one answer to a question that persists.

There exists the ultimate natural powers working in favour of us and according to our needs. Let's just understand it and be vulnerable enough to accept and understand the working of the same. The mere realisation and acceptance would bring you magical differences in your life if you notice the patterns carefully.

There is a lot more in life, we could ever understand in this lifetime but what we can accept is the way how it unfolds in front of us with a heart full of gratitude and compassion.

The only super power that stays immortal out of any mortal living being is their attitude of gratitude.

Be clear and mindful of the fact that the titles, popularity and success are just the returns of universe favours to you for being grateful and compassionate.

Have you noticed ever, that the more you wait for something to happen, the more time it takes to be done for you.

When things change inside you, things change outside you.

There comes many a times in my life when I feel like after doing every possible thing, I cannot make it up to what I want, which leave me feel miserable about myself and my condition of not being able to do anything. I feel the end of the world, literally. But with all the self-help books and self-help people (For me, that's my parents, my sister and my best friend) who does the literal magic to turn on the magic lying inside of me to turn out the best of everything that I can do or am supposed to do. This is what everyone needs to understand about the situations where you cannot help yourself but the nature is supporting you by either of the ways, always.

I am not any sort of professional writer but yes you could see me as a heartfelt writer who writes what she feels or what she has encountered in life.

The magical experiences of mine are infinite but I am letting you know about what brought me such experiences to grab your part of the best ones in this lifetime.

The practices to be followed in full discipline is quite tough but serves the best of everything you dream of.

The dream of achieving anything lies completely on your wish and will.

But to give it a start, note your dream down somewhere just like we sow a seed of our choice to get the plant respectively. And once you write it with full confidence, the universe says – your wish is my command. And all the circumstances will be set to help you out to achieve your dream. It's all about 20% efforts and 80% trust on yourself and universe or you can call it as Mother Nature to work for you.

AS BELIEVED – GENUINE EFFORTS NEVER GO WASTE.

The belief is what makes us different, greater and let us know about our own higher self.

The higher self means –

WHAT ARE OUR CAPABILITIES?

WHAT ARE OUR SKILLS?

WHAT ARE OUR PROS?

WHAT ARE THE WAYS WE CAN HELP OUR SELVES AND OTHERS?

WHAT ARE THE WAYS TO COPE UP WITH ANY SITUATION IN ANY ASPECT OF LIFE?

AND THE MOST IMPORTANT REALISATION –

HOW BLESSED WE ARE IN ALL ASPECTS OF LIFE!

WITHOUT ANY DOUBT

You can write here to know your true higher self and recognize your real potential.

Just close your eyes, breathe in and out for 2-5 minutes, take a pen and start answering these questions. You'll really feel empowered after reading your own answers.

MY CAPABILITIES

____

____

____

____

MY SKILLS

____

____

____

____

MY PROS (ADVANTAGES)

____

____

____

____

MY CONS (DISADVANTAGES)

____

____

____

____

WAYS OF HELPING MY OWN SELF AND OTHERS (IT MAY BE OF ANY KIND)

WAYS TO COPE UP IN ANY SITUATIONS LIFE THROWS AT ME

LIST OF THINGS I AM BLESSED WITH

(THIS LIST IS KIND OF INFINITE)

But just to make you understand how blessed you are.

To have a guru in life is
to have a lifetime subscription of wisdom
and grace.

— Bhav9_thefeels

DEVOTION IS AN INVESTMENT FOR A BETTER LIFE

I GOT TO KNOW THIS WHEN I EXPERIENCED THE SAME.

PRACTICING DEVOTION IN ANY FORM AND AT ANY PLACE CAN HEAL YOU EVEN WHEN YOU DON'T KNOW ABOUT WHICH PARTS NEEDED TO BE HEALED.

Today I found a great quote that should be treasured for life by j. iron word – "IN A WORLD, WHERE WE ARE LOSING OURSELVES TO TECHNOLOGY, LOVE IS THE LAST TRUE THING WE HAVE LEFT."

Love and devotion goes hand in hand.

And I learnt that when I experienced something people literally crave for.

I met MY GURUDEV – SRI SRI RAVISHANKAR.

It was all a result of love, devotion and resolution.

Life literally takes unexpected turns to make you reach at the right destination at the right time.

Everything falls into the right place if you decide and surrender to the universe.

I just made this year's resolution to meet gurudev. I did not knew how and when it was going to happen, I just made my mind and set my intention with all the love and trust.

One fine day in the month of February, I got a call from my uncle asking me to join him for the Art of living International Ashram, Bangalore for meeting Gurudev. And without any second thoughts I said YES.

THIS YES GOT ME THE MOST AMAZING DAY WHEN I MET GURUDEV.

The happiness with the tears in my eyes, I shouted – I LOVE YOU, GURUDEV.

That moment of love, devotion and prayer altogether is a once in a lifetime experience people wish for.

I received this blessing by being grateful and confident on the thought of meeting gurudev.

Devotion is just a form of love towards the god that could take you to another level of spirituality which is crucial now a days.

As Gurudev says –A person in love with the divine makes others also like that. Whatever is there within you that is what others receive and that is what you perceive in others.

Spirituality is one of the key investments needed and to be done to lead a peaceful life. And since its trending, you will want to add it to your lifestyle. As pleasure simply lies here.

To be hopeful means
to know everything
will be done in your favour,
no matter how and when.

— Bhav9_thefeels

BE HOPEFUL, NO MATTER WHAT. (BECAUSE YOU'RE ALWAYS SUPPORTED AND PROTECTED)

In today's life, we are stuck in feeling of lack, no matter how much we have. To believe that we have enough is the key to be hopeful, no matter what. I've walked through moments when hope felt like it was slipping away and my everything seemed to fall apart. But even in the darkest times, holding on to prayer, belief, and trust made all the difference. When you keep faith in your hopes, life eventually aligns in ways you never expected. Sooner or later, it happens—because it actually and finally happened for me. That unwavering trust will let you pass any situation till your hopes gets fulfilled, it may be of any kind or matter.

Adding to this, if you think about the odds and evens of any situation where you think that nothing will work after putting every kind of energy, just get your energy back and keep it inside your heart. Stop making efforts, stop sending signals. Simply, channelize your energy in believing that you got this. (Whatever you're hoping for) And start making room for the same. Since, the timing for receiving we've been asking for depends on the divine not us. And trusting that you're guided, supported and protected by the divine makes the process of waiting easier. Take glory in knowing that you are hopeful because you're definitely going to be rewarded, at the right time, in the right way. As the divine's timing is perfect, always.

In this whole process, you might loose hope, you might get confused about your decision, and you might get hurt too. But the belief, the unwavering belief that your hope will turn into the reality will definitely make it come true. Your time, energy and trust will never go in vain. And that is for sure.

Also, this book is the biggest example of the same. Because years of experiencing, reading, writing and many more such aspects with the most crucial element – 'BEING HOPEFUL' turned my dream of being a published author, a reality.

I hope and pray, may you understand to give the lead of your life to love, gratitude, devotion, prayers and blessings.

And may you receive the same patience, kindness, understanding and love you give to others.

CONGRATULATIONS ON RECEIVING THE ULTIMATE KNOWLEDGE AND POWER TO LEAD A LIFE EVERYONE CRAVES AND WISHES FOR.

MANIFESTING AN ABUNDANT LIFE FOR ALL MY READERS....

DECLARATION

While every effort has been made to ensure the accuracy and reliability of the information presented in this book, it is important to note that the author does not claim ownership of any external materials, references, or works not specifically created by them. Any sources, quotes, or ideas used have been included for educational purposes, and all attempts have been made to provide proper attribution where applicable.

If any copyrighted material has been used inadvertently or without proper permission, it was unintentional and not meant to infringe upon any rights. The author encourages readers to contact them directly for any corrections or clarifications regarding such matters.

The contents of this book are intended as general guidance and not as professional advice. The author and publisher cannot be held liable for any actions taken based on the information provided.

Thank you for understanding.

The author can be found on LinkedIn and Facebook,
and on Instagram as @bhav9_thefeels

THANK-YOU ONCE AGAIN ☺